7 MINDSETS TO SUCCESSFULLY TRANSITION FROM EMPLOYEE TO ENTREPRENEUR

Jason S. Murray

JOURNAL JOY

An *Imprint* of Journal Joy *Publishers*
www.thejournaljoy.com

CONTENTS

DEDICATION... 1

FOREWORD... 4

INTRODUCTION 8

CHAPTER ONE: Steps From Employee To Entrepreneur 11

CHAPTER TWO: Challenges and Rewards of Being an
entrepreneur 26

CHAPTER THREE: Steps For Entrepreneurs To Obtain
Capital To Launch A Business 38

CHAPTER FOUR: Types of Businesses and Industries That
Can Succeed... 43

CHAPTER FIVE: Developing Your Team (Mastermind) of
Advisors 61

CHAPTER SIX: Interviews of Successful Entrepreneurs 68

Entrepreneur's Spotlight: 82

CHAPTER SEVEN: Descriptions and How to Create
Budgets/Marketing/Profit Forecasting/Business
Plan/Competitive Analysis 89

CHAPTER EIGHT: Conclusion 97

AUTHOR BIO.. 103

RESOURCES 105

DEDICATION

This is my third publication, and I would like to dedicate this book to several individuals who are important to me and have assisted in the development of my ever-evolving legacy.

My wife, Tanya Moore-Murray, whom I've known for over 40 years and have been married to for 28 years, nurturing our family and providing our children and grandchildren an example of togetherness and perseverance as a couple.

My mother, Elizabeth Murray, who gave me a foundation early in life to understand fiscal responsibility and the importance of managing life skills, while simultaneously being an example of a caring parent, providing unwavering love and support.

My children, Imani Murray (Morgan), Jabari Murray (Samantha), Khalia Murray (Brandon), T. Amiyra King (Jarrod), Shariyf Lester (Chavonne), and Rayhaan Lester, who have shown my wife and me that our commitment for raising respected, responsible adults has been realized. Their commitment to raising their respective families with a foundation of love, discipline, and provisions of knowledge of their family heritage is being fulfilled.

My grandchildren, Lauren Lester, Jamarieux Murray, Nia Murray, Tamia Jackson Murray, Aspen King, Olivia Murray, Carter Lester, Chandler King, Ruel Lester, Layla Murray, and Gianna Murray, who continue to provide me with inspiration to focus on what's important in life, which is family, health, and legacy.

My brothers, B. Desmond Murray, aka Bakari Adeyemi, who continues to influence me with his commitment to excellence and professionalism; Darryl Hicks, who provides me with inspiration as a successful entrepreneur; and Ram Fishburne, who works diligently to keep our family together and share precious memories through his photography skills. Additionally, my sister, Angela Davis, who became family while we were college classmates and continues her unwavering love and support for our family through her genuine personality.

My parents in love, Elaine, and Gilbert Moore, who give from the heart and share their time to provide support for our family in many ways.

And lastly, my ancestors: father, James Murray, Jr.; grandparents, Nettie and Harrison Bradley; grandparents, Sarah and James Murray, Sr., who are looking over us and were responsible for giving my parents life, who ultimately gave me life, enabling me to become the individual I am through administering my God-given talents.

FOREWORD

By Nichelle Santos

Jason Murray has created a roadmap for a viable path forward, to break away from the daily grind and belief system of working hard for someone else, or a corporation, as the only path to success; to an awakening and transformation of the mindset, to transition from employee to an entrepreneur; to own your business and control your destiny. His "must read" book, "7 Mindsets to Successfully Transition from Employee to Entrepreneur", I believe, will bring a new frontier of business owners and entrepreneurship to reduce the wealth gap; increase homeownership; increase and enhance education opportunities; increase political influence; and so much more, to have a transgenerational impact.

The COVID-19 Pandemic has caused in our society a cultural shift, "The Mass Resignation", as schools and employment became virtual, eliminating the necessity and stress of the grueling commute; leaving only essential workers as necessary to perform responsibilities in person. During this remote revolution, society had the opportunity to reflect on priorities, family, and happiness. They learned how to value their own time and flexibility, their worth, and well-being, with a desire to earn more money. Many realized what they truly desired would be unattainable in working for someone else. As a result, millions never returned to their positions, creating massive labor shortages and a demand for higher wages. What this remote revolution has created is a renaissance for entrepreneurialism.

According to data from the Bureau of Labor Statistics, 20% of new businesses fail during the first two years of being open, 45% during the first five years, and 65% during the first ten years. Only 25% of new businesses make it to 15 years or more, a daunting statistic. So, allow this information to serve as a warning that entrepreneurship is not easy; it requires great sacrifice: blood, sweat and tears; but offers the rewards, flexibility, and pride that only ownership brings, if and only if, you are prepared for the journey.

Entrepreneurship is a mindset of autonomy and leadership; it can be naturally attained or acquired. In my case it was naturally attained and organically acquired. My mother, Marie Santos was an entrepreneur, and my father, Ted, worked a 9-5. I witnessed firsthand the success, and sometimes failure, of the variety of businesses my mother attempted, as an art dealer, real estate broker, and even Mary Kay. I recall periods of time when she had flexibility in her schedule to be with the family more, and the contrast, the lack of availability, when she did work in a corporate role.

I quickly learned that I liked having my own money from about age 7. I received an allowance if I did my chores around the house or played with my younger sister. By age 10, I was cooking, cleaning, helping with homework, and doing my sister's hair before school; I was also a "Safety Patrol" in the 4th and 5th grades at Asher Holmes Elementary School.

My neighborhood was a close-knit community, in the suburbs of Marlboro, NJ. The other moms noticed my mature, responsible behavior and asked my mother if I could babysit their children, and even bring my sister. Getting paid $3.00 - $5.00/hr. by age 12 was impactful to me and helped to launch me into entrepreneurship; I even shared wages with my sister.

I learned my worth at an early age; what also helped shape my young mind was the dedication to excel as a track and field athlete, with the discipline of practice for higher rate of return on performance. Unfortunately, I lost both parents when I was just 16 years old, and independence became a necessity, in addition to my desire. I continued my education and athletics at Rutgers University; and eventually at Harvard as well; however, I treated my experience in corporate America as continued education to learn the process of business; and as a vehicle to transport and transform me from employee to the purpose driven, serial entrepreneur and businesswoman I am today.

INTRODUCTION

Entrepreneurship isn't for everyone; however, those who can succeed as entrepreneurs are able to reap tremendous rewards. As the path to entrepreneurship has its challenges and rewards, the cycle to a successful path is filled with many life-changing experiences. Giving the ability to learn and put into practice fundamental principles of business gives an individual an incredible foundation for making an impact in society and fosters tremendous examples for our current generation and future generations. I was fortunate to learn about business in college and earn a degree, then implement what I learned in the corporate world.

I then transitioned to become a successful entrepreneur after developing a foundation of business success through the path of an extensive sales and marketing career. It should certainly, be noted that the path to rise through a corporate ladder to the CEO level in business is usually through the sales and marketing channel. Subsequently, when one succeeds as an entrepreneur or business owner, an individual is, in most cases, a superior sales professional with an understanding of how business works and how to develop a marketing plan, then execute a well-defined business plan.

The goal of this book is to provide insights for individuals who are aspiring to become successful entrepreneurs after spending time working for someone else, then deciding that it's time to develop a business of their own and executing an exit strategy from a well-paying job or a job where the individual is unsatisfied with their career. They want more and are ready for the challenges and rewards of entrepreneurship.

Whether an individual stays in the corporate environment or branches out to succeed in business through entrepreneurial endeavors, one must be focused on identifying problems, developing solutions, and determining the best way to distribute their product or service to the masses who will benefit from the solutions that are developed.

The goal of the entrepreneur is to build their business and scale their business to a point where they can either generate consistent profits for years into the future or build a successful enterprise, develop an exit strategy to sell their business, and then develop additional enterprises by modeling the success from their first enterprise. Having a vision for developing a business begins with an idea, followed by market research and suitability analysis, and then developing an in-depth business plan, providing the entrepreneur with action steps to start, own, and operate a successful business.

CHAPTER ONE

STEPS FROM EMPLOYEE TO ENTREPRENEUR

"I built a conglomerate and emerged the richest black man in the world in 2008, but it didn't happen overnight. It took me 30 years to get to where I am today. Youths of today aspire to be like me, but they want to achieve it overnight. It's not going to work. To build a successful business, you must start small and dream big. In the journey of entrepreneurship, tenacity of purpose is supreme."

— Aliko Dangote

We have been taught to focus most of our energy towards developing an ability to earn an income through a salary to take care of ourselves and our families by going to school, obtaining a job, and then leading a successful career based on developing job skills, trade skills, or using our creative abilities to earn wages. Additionally, individuals who are artistic or have athletic abilities or entertainment talents can lead their lives by entertaining the public and earn enormous sums of wages depending on their respective skill levels. In previous generations decades ago, the emphasis was placed more on business skills, developing a craft, or farming skills in the early part of the 1900s. As we can see, times have changed tremendously. With the major emphasis on obtaining job skills as opposed to creating jobs, most individuals gear their career paths in the direction of working for someone else and earning a salary as opposed to creating a salary through self-employment or entrepreneurial endeavors. So, who makes the decision to think beyond most people? I would say, it's the individual who is driven to make a difference and excel with their ability to impact the lives of many.

Education from grade school, middle school, and high school is mandatory in this country, and the foundation set forth in our educational system provides individuals an opportunity to understand how to function in society, interact with people, and earn wages to lead a quality life. Therefore, one can argue that obtaining an education in this society is the fundamental foundation for accessing the lifestyle of one's choice. This fundamental foundation gives individuals a start in life; however, we encourage further studies beyond high school to position ourselves to earn higher wages during our lifetimes because obtaining the basic high school education is perceived to not be enough for most individuals to have a superior lifestyle in our society. Obtaining higher levels of education or specialized training gives individuals a perceived increased advantage over the individual who merely obtains the mandatory level of education.

As the rising cost of education continues to escalate, who is benefiting from the high costs of education? Are the students benefiting the most, or the educational institutions who place a high premium on education to prepare individuals in our society to earn higher wages? This can certainly be debatable; however, we want to look at what is most important. We also place a high premium on entertainment in our society; therefore, athletes and entertainers are paid millions to perform and entertain the public based on their ability to develop their talents to professional levels. There lies a disconnect because an athlete or entertainer doesn't have to obtain continuous higher education to increase their income potential; however, to succeed in a job in the corporate world, higher education, or public service, one must, in most cases, achieve graduate level degrees or additional specialized training to qualify for higher pay or leadership positions in our workforce.

Then, we must look at the lack of education most entertainers and athletes, for the most part, have regarding financial education or business skills, which would give them the ability to leverage the large sums of money they make for a short period of time in their professional lives and careers. The average length of an athlete's or entertainer's career is much shorter than that of an employee who works for a corporation during their lifetime. We can see where our emphasis on certain areas perhaps should be shifted to provide all individuals with information and necessary education to succeed in protecting their livelihoods, taking care of their families, and leading productive lives.

In my opinion, the first step for an individual to shift from an employee to an entrepreneur is obtaining the necessary education through either book knowledge or theory about business and hands-on training in the business world. The success of an employee in their job function, whether they are an individual producer, manager, or high-level executive leading and managing a large group of employees, will determine their level of success as an entrepreneur or business owner. My experience working in corporate America spanned three decades, and I worked in many industries, primarily as an individual producer in the sales and marketing channel.

Those experiences gave me a clear understanding of the sales function and the importance of good marketing strategies, as well as the discipline to meet and exceed quotas to drive business and increase my income. As I transitioned in my professional sales career from various jobs and industries, I always looked to obtain a higher paying job with additional benefits or perks, which kept me striving for more and to continue succeeding in my career. If I failed to meet quota or provide the adequate progression in my role as a sales professional, life for me in my career would become stressful. As an employee earning a salary, benefits, and perks, such as a company car and a flexible schedule, one must be sure to make and exceed quota to stay employed and in good standing with a corporate employer. One of the advantages of a sales career is that your role is directly aligned with profits and revenue generation. With the capacity to keep your company profitable based on your activity and production, your job security is better positioned compared to other employees, whose roles and responsibilities are geared towards operations, human resources, or non-revenue-generating activities.

When an employee makes the decision to transition to entrepreneurship, I believe that's when he or she develops a vision to make a difference, seeks to grow as an individual through their vision, or clearly understands what they are truly passionate about through visualizing their true purpose. I can recall that I wanted to become an author and write a book about the importance of fatherhood. It was my vision to make a difference and show others the rewards of being a great father and taking on the full responsibility of what fatherhood represents. My goal was to encourage individuals that taking full ownership of their role as a father would benefit them, their families, and their communities. The impact of my vision drove me to research the best way to become an author and publish my first book. I subsequently was offered the opportunity to be a co-author of a publication, which allowed me to further make an impact through writing and sharing my story through my second book.

My vision to become an entrepreneur and lead a successful business was fostered during my experience as a group subscription sales manager for *Black Enterprise Magazine.* Working for one of the true legends in business and entrepreneurship, Mr. Earl Graves, Sr., and Earl Graves Publishing gave me the awareness of what developing a business, growing a business, and the rewards and challenges of entrepreneurship truly represented. As I studied and read the stories of successful business enterprises featured in *Black Enterprise Magazine* while simultaneously selling group subscriptions of the magazine to large organizations across the country, I began to dream of one day being a successful entrepreneur myself. It led me to continue developing my skills as a sales professional; however, it also lit a fire in me to see myself as a business owner fulfilling my desire to succeed in business.

That vision has been realized, as I've been an entrepreneur for over a decade and have sustained myself in business through ups, downs, and uncertainty in the markets at times during those years. The question I believe is important for all individuals to ask themselves is, "What is your vision for your life and purpose?"

Most businesses are built by identifying a problem or uncovering a need of the masses, and then developing a solution to that problem or satisfying an unmet need. As an individual thinks of ways to go into business by becoming an entrepreneur, a driving force is usually understanding that a change is necessary due to current unfavorable conditions or that a demand for a product or service will make a difference; or, a new trend emerges in our society, and an aspiring entrepreneur identifies and capitalizes on the new trend by fulfilling the new demand. Thus, it is my opinion that there are solutions for all problems, and the individual who can identify problems and develop solutions to those problems on a large scale can realize wealth through business formation and execution of solutions by supplying the goods or services to fulfill the demand.

I believe that a second step in the transition process from employee to entrepreneur is determining that your current income isn't sufficient to cover your current expenses to lead the life you want to lead. As we live in a capitalistic society, the rise in the cost of living puts tremendous pressure on individuals to get ahead in life. While going to school to get an education to earn a living is recommended, the return on the investment doesn't always translate to a high-paying job to adequately put an individual in a position to start a family, purchase a home, and save for our children's college education. So, we have a cycle that needs changing. If we have student loan debt, which takes years to pay off, can we begin to invest and save for retirement, start a family, and purchase a home to build wealth simultaneously?

Working in a platform that has a cap on your earning potential leads many individuals to say to themselves, "There must be a better way to increase my earning power and, at the same time, develop multiple streams of income to position myself for a better quality of life and enable myself to provide additional resources for my family." Thus, working in a job situation as opposed to starting a business with unlimited income potential can delay individuals' quest for starting a family, and they decide it's best to stay single for a long period of time. Even if someone decides to stay single and enjoy themselves during their young adult life, without adequate financial resources, an individual won't be able to travel, experience lavish entertainment venues, or lead a lifestyle of consistent dating for socialization.

There are several ways an individual can earn an income. As an employee, an individual receives a W-2 and usually pays more taxes. If you develop self-employment income as a doctor, dentist, or lawyer, you must acquire specialized training, earning credentials in your specialized field, which requires enormous time and financial resources or scholarships to obtain. In this platform, you don't have leverage of your time, meaning if you don't provide a service, you won't get paid. On the other hand, if you develop a business and hire employees to work for you or with you, you create leverage by utilizing others to produce the goods and services you market, and you create opportunities to scale your business through collaborative efforts of others. Lastly, if you generate income through investments, you leverage your money and allow compound interest over a period to increase the value of your investments; thus, you leverage your financial resources adequately and efficiently.

Entrepreneurs and business owners develop skills to succeed in business through different paths. As the transition from employee to entrepreneur gives an individual an opportunity to work for themselves and create jobs, a person can develop leadership skills through volunteering in professional organizations that they may have experience in based on the industry they work in. I was fortunate to develop a variety of skills by being a member of National Sales Network, an organization of African American sales professionals and sales managers whose mission is to meet the professional and developmental needs of sales professionals and sales management professionals and individuals. The organization was founded in Newark, New Jersey in 1992, has various chapters across the country, and recently celebrated 30 years as an organization developing talented sales managers and sales professionals across the country.

As I became a member and subsequently a leader serving in various capacities within the New Jersey/New York chapter, I developed platform skills, public speaking skills, and overall leadership skills, which assisted me as a corporate sales professional. This skills development also assisted me in my transition from a successful corporate career to a successful entrepreneur in business in the financial services industry. In the transition from working to meet quota in a competitive selling environment for many years to having to gain a different level of discipline in your approach to business as an entrepreneur or business owner, you must create goals and make revenue accumulation and growth of your business your major priorities.

Determining what goals to establish and what revenue will be necessary to develop a profitable business of your own is much different from being directed what to do and what goals and objectives to meet.

Another organization that I became a member of is the Association of African American Financial Advisors, which was created to address the needs and concerns of African American financial professionals. The goal of the organization is to foster the value of financial planning and advance the financial planning professional. The Association of African American Financial Advisors just celebrated 20 years of existence and is looking forward to growing as an organization. Both organizations assisted me in improving my skills as an overall professional and, more importantly, gave me the opportunity to give back to my community and serve as a mentor to many sales professionals and financial professionals who were starting out in their respective careers and seeking guidance from individuals who have developed careers and lead businesses.

Becoming an entrepreneur isn't for everyone. An indication of that is many businesses who open and last more than three to five years are sole proprietors. If they don't get to a point where they can hire employees to assist with the growth and development of their business, yes, they are business owners; however, an entrepreneur who is able to start a business and develop their business into a business enterprise with employees, thus scaling their business, can truly be looked upon as a successful entrepreneur.

Some of the characteristics of a successful entrepreneur are that they are an individual who is creative and possesses leadership skills, analytical skills, and strong people skills. These characteristics are just a snapshot view of a successful entrepreneur, and there are certainly many more. There is one train of thought that indicates entrepreneurs are born with certain skills to succeed as business owners, and the other train of thought is that entrepreneurs must develop those characteristics and skills to succeed in business.

A recent compilation of findings regarding small business ownership in the U.S. is:

• Small businesses make up 99.9% of all U.S. businesses, but a minority of the workforce.

• Women- and minority-owned businesses still lag far behind firms owned by white men.

- Women-owned businesses have skyrocketed by 114% over the past 20 years; however, the revenue share of women-owned businesses has fallen .02% in that same period

- Most entrepreneurs did not possess a college degree.

- Minority-owned businesses were less likely to attract outside funding. Source: U.S. Small Business Administration

Whether a business has one employee or many employees, to successfully grow and maintain a profitable business, the ownership must be tenacious, driven for achieving sustainable activities, and focused on persistently seeking ways to satisfy their customer base continuously. This is all accomplished by developing a sound business plan that is comprehensive, based on market data and a competitive analysis, and tailored to meet the needs and objectives of the client base or customers who will be loyal supporters of the business entity in a substantial way. The business plan will be the start; however, to expand the business, there will be a necessity to adjust the plan according to the market conditions, trends in the industry the business is in, and the changing landscape of the competition entering the same marketplace.

Some solid advice I would recommend for employees making the transition from employee to entrepreneur while developing their business plan to open a business, from a financial standpoint, is to develop a savings fund for your business, separate from an amount designated for your emergency fund. Additionally, an account should be established to ensure you can put food on the table and pay rent or mortgage for nine months to a year before you make the transition. It is optimal to keep your day job if you can while developing a ramp-up period of your business, at the same time avoiding any conflicts of interest between your current employment and your aspiring business venture.

During the ramp-up period, you want to pay down your debts and get rid of your car note. As you free up money to pursue your business, be sure to invest in your personal development to ensure you possess the mental toughness to succeed as an entrepreneur. Another area you should focus on is cutting your living expenses before making the transition, as this will allow you to develop a budget based on your current expenditures with the anticipation that during the ramp-up period, you will have to adjust until the business revenue begins to increase. Lastly, you want to focus on keeping good records of your expenses without commingling your personal income with your business income as you make the transition, as this will give you a clear understanding of your business revenue's trajectory and what direction it is scaling.

Questions aspiring entrepreneurs should answer:

1. What am I good at?

2. What am I passionate about?

3. What will the future trends in society represent?

4. What problems exist in the world?

5. How can I make a difference to impact the lives of others?

6. What are my strengths?

7. Who has the most purchasing power in our society?

8. What products or services are in demand currently, and which ones will be in demand in the future?

9. Who makes most buying decisions?

10. How does supply and demand create business growth?

11.Do I want to work for myself, or continue to build someone else's dream? 12. How can I develop a business plan?

CHAPTER TWO

CHALLENGES AND REWARDS OF BEING AN ENTREPRENEUR

"Aspiring entrepreneurs have to do something that they feel strongly passionate about, and in most cases, they should seek inspiration from their own experience. If you had a terrible experience, you should despise the experience to the extent that you are continuously seeking a solution for it."

— Best Ayiorwoth

Entrepreneurship has its challenges, rewards, and memorable moments. When an individual decides on a path to develop entrepreneurial endeavors, he or she must understand that the road to success can be an up-and-down situation. What is also important for individuals pursuing their goal to achieve success as an entrepreneur to understand is that failure and obstacles are a part of the process. The ability to manage your expectations during the path to succeed with business ownership is paramount. Additionally, having faith that you will succeed is essential.

For most entrepreneurs, raising capital or securing an initial investment to start a business is one of the most challenging aspects of business startups. Also, an entrepreneur must create a solid business plan with the proper research through comprehensive competitive analysis, market analysis, and a thorough product/service analysis, coupled with solid financial fundamentals. Generating a profit for a business owner within three to five years is probably the most significant challenge a business owner must overcome. Data from the Bureau of Labor Statistics shows that approximately 20% of new businesses fail during the first two years of being open, 45% during the first five years, and 65% during the first 10 years. Only 25% of new businesses make it to 15 years or more. Three to four years is the standard estimation for how long it takes a business to be profitable. Most of your earnings in the first year of the business will be used for paying expenses and reinvestment.

One solution to overcome the challenge of securing capital to start a business is to find a platform with a low capital entry point and, at the same time, have tremendous upside potential by making a commitment to follow the steps necessary to succeed within the business model or platform.

Business Failure Rate Across the U.S.

Time frame Percentage of businesses that fail

Within 1 year

18.4%

After 2 years

30.6%

After 3 years

37.9%

After 4 years

44.5%

After 5 years

49.7%

After 6 years

53.6%

After 7 years

56.8%

After 8 years

60.5%

After 9 years

63.4%

After 10 years

65.5%

Source: LendingTree analysis of U.S. Bureau of Labor Statistics data

I'm happy to share that my initial startup cost for my financial services business was less than $1,000. As I developed my business, there were additional costs that I had to incur to stay in business and increase my ability to expand my business by obtaining additional licenses in various states and maintaining the necessary insurance, annual fees, and biannual license renewal fees. Additionally, when I opened my own office after working out of an office of my business partner and paying some of the costs for the lease payment in the office, I had to incur additional expenses of my own to maintain my office. What's important to note is that I had generated years of revenue from my practice to now pay for my office space, which I've had since 2015. Thus, I have a profitable business that started in 2010 and continues to expand. Another factor I will point out is that I received my securities licenses (Series 7 and Series 66) while being an employee of Merrill Lynch in 2007 during a paid training program; thus, I successfully transitioned from being an employee in the financial services industry to becoming a successful entrepreneur in the financial services industry for over 10 years.

The last challenge I will mention regarding making a transition from employee to entrepreneur is determining your purpose of opening a business and how that purpose is in alignment with the purpose of your life. When your purpose in business is in alignment with your purpose in life, there is nothing that can stop you from succeeding. An individual can have a desire to succeed in business *and* develop a business plan for the creation of the business. An entrepreneur must be very passionate about the industry, have an idea of the solutions the business will provide, and know the impact the business will have on society. When all these factors are in alignment with one's purpose-driven life, the ability to sustain a profitable business and expand the business exponentially will successfully be achieved.

A banker raised me, and early on in life, I was exposed to money management skills by watching my parent successfully manage bills, raise a family, and successfully send me and my brother to college while she simultaneously began saving for her retirement. That example encouraged me to take the same approach when I started a family and led me to eventually pursue a career in the financial services industry, then ultimately become an entrepreneur, assisting others to manage money, grow and protect their assets, and secure their financial futures. Thus, my business is in alignment with my purpose-driven life, as it's been what I've learned and been enthusiastic about, and it's in alignment with what skills I'm incredibly good at. The correlation with purpose, passion, and skill set provides an entrepreneur a foundation that can be built upon as the entrepreneur weathers storms, develops a business, and ultimately provides jobs for others through the creation and expansion of a business enterprise.

As challenges and obstacles stand in the way of an entrepreneur and the entrepreneur subsequently overcomes the challenges and obstacles, the rewards and benefits of entrepreneurship will surface. As stated earlier, if the individual pursuing the journey and life of an entrepreneur can manage his/her expectations throughout the journey to successful entrepreneurial endeavors, then the satisfaction of achievement is incredible. I can recall when I first took my Series 7 exam to become a licensed professional in the securities business, I failed my test by two points. Yes, I needed a 70 to obtain my license, and I received a 68. What a deflating feeling to have when I came so close. So, what did I have to do? I had to buckle down, put in extra hours of studying, and make sure to focus on securing my license the next time I took my test. The consequence of not passing meant that I would have lost my job at Merrill Lynch, as they usually give individuals one chance to pass the Series 7 exam. I was fortunate to get a second chance, and I wasn't about to lose my opportunity to establish myself as a licensed professional in the financial services industry.

Some of the rewards of successful entrepreneurial endeavors and business ownership consists of unlimited income, satisfaction of making a difference, creating jobs, solving problems, and making an impact on society. When one makes an impact on society, they develop influence, especially when they are considered an expert in their field or a thought leader in industry. I've been fortunate to learn from experts in my career, and I've been mentored by legends in industry. The reward and benefit for me from those experiences is that it provided me with a foundation for success and, at the same time, gave me the examples needed for me to see from others what I can now do for myself, as well as serve as an example for others who watch my success in business.

When I discovered what I was good at, I focused my attention on getting better at my sales and marketing skills, along with my ability to get along with people and develop persuasive techniques as a business professional. While succeeding in the corporate world gave me a sense of satisfaction, I knew that as I wanted to take my skill set to the next level by earning my income as opposed to receiving a salary for wages, I must develop additional skills to do so. Thus, I began to read about successful entrepreneurs and thought leaders in the business world and sought out additional mentorship from successful business professionals. What these actions gave me was a further sense of belief that my ability to succeed as an entrepreneur was in my reach. Therefore, it's rewarding to know that your goal to pursue entrepreneurial endeavors begins with a thought. Then, you must back it up with action, persistence, and an unwavering ability to focus and stay focused along the journey.

Business ownership, when successfully designed, built, and maximized creates wealth for the business owner. In many cases, a business owner will have partners or other business associates who work together to grow their company. As the collaboration of business partners is fulfilled and business enterprises are developed, the rewards and benefits are expanded to the communities in which the companies have their headquarters or their regional and local offices. By providing goods, products, or services through business expansion, the clients who are loyal to the business with their ongoing consumption benefit as well through the goods and services that are consumed or utilized. Creating jobs in our society through small business ownership is the backbone of our society. The development of a large corporation is optimal, yet it requires an enormous amount of planning, dedication, and perseverance to reach multi-million-dollar revenue status.

The U.S. has a lot of **small businesses**—more than 30 million, in fact. But despite there being so many, a small minority of large firms swallows up most of the wealth. And while 99.9% of all businesses in the U.S. are classified as small businesses, they employ less than half of the workforce— 47.3%, or 59.9 million people, **according to 2019 U.S. Small Business Administration statistics**.

Most startup founders tend to be in their 40s, according to this graph. Image source: Author

Developing a legacy through business ownership is one of the most rewarding experiences for an entrepreneur. Let's think about this. Let's say an entrepreneur opens a business, generates profits to add additional employees to the business, then expands the business to other states, and the business becomes a national business. With the national success of the business, the prospect of expanding the business to other countries is presented to the business operation; thus, now, the business is an international business entity. The creation of this business from an idea, a business plan, and the execution of a sound marketing strategy to enact the business plan has now created a business corporation on a global level. This, in turn, can allow the legacy of the business owner or founder of the company to have his or her impact in the world passed down to their next generation. The key point here, though, is that the founder's children would have to want to pursue working in the business, learning the business, and keeping the business in the family name. This can be a challenge, as not all children of business owners have the same vision and passion to run the family business, even if it's successful. Some children of successful business owners want an identity of their own or want to develop their own entrepreneurial endeavors.

My first book, *Faith + Purpose = Legacy*, was intended to encourage our children to become entrepreneurs and learn through the example that parents can show children. My belief is that children follow what their parents do in most cases, as opposed to what their parents say to do. Therefore, when children of entrepreneurs see a successful path of achievement through entrepreneurial endeavors, it increases the chance they will follow their parents' path. What's important to note, in my opinion, is that if the children decide to develop their own paths to success, that's all right. The major outcome is that they succeed in life, regardless of whether they follow their parents' footsteps or develop a path of their own to success.

An additional reward to becoming a successful entrepreneur is the time you get back to have independence of your activities. The time factor is critical when considering the time necessary to put in for the purpose of building a business. Once the business is built, an entrepreneur then has provided themselves with an ability to do as he or she pleases because the cash flow and revenue generating activities have increased and are sustainable. When an abundance of financial resources is no longer an issue, an individual can then travel, spend time with his or her family, and begin to implement philanthropic activities.

Questions individuals should answer are:

1. What determines my level of success?

2. How can I determine what I'm good at?

3. What activities will give me an understanding of business acumen?

4. Which organizations provide business mentorship?

5. Can I succeed as an entrepreneur today in society?

CHAPTER THREE

STEPS FOR ENTREPRENEURS TO OBTAIN CAPITAL TO LAUNCH A BUSINESS

"The battles that count aren't the ones for gold medals. The struggles within yourself—the invisible, inevitable battles inside all of us—that's where it's at."

— Jesse Owens

Developing a business plan to start a business is a foundation to prepare for the business to open. To start the business, capital is necessary to open the doors of the business. Whether your business is located at a traditional brick-and-mortar location, or clients can access your products or services online, there are certain costs associated with business formation.

Obtaining the capital to start a business requires an entrepreneur to carefully analyze what the best source of obtaining the capital for a business enterprise is, as there are advantages and disadvantages to the various capital sources. Some examples of sources of startup capital are personal savings, venture capitalists, angel investors, business loans through banks, family and friends, and your personal 401K plan. The U.S. Small Business Administration is an excellent resource to utilize to get advice on capital startup costs. According to the U.S. Small Business Administration, most micro-businesses cost around $3,000 to start, while most home-based franchises cost $2,000 to $5,000. If an individual is interested in opening a franchise, the capital necessary to open a franchise would be a lot more and could range from $30,000 to $500,000, or even more.

The most common startup expenses are office rental space, office furniture, basic technology, insurance, advertising, marketing, website and hosting costs, and labor costs. Depending on whether you plan to have employees or independent contractors when you initially open your business will determine the range of your labor costs. It's important to understand that your costs will vary; however, there will be some fixed costs associated with the business. Then, your expenses overall will fluctuate depending on the products and services you are marketing to your prospective clients.

Utilizing your personal savings would be an ideal source for starting a business because you wouldn't have to be concerned with paying any money back with interest. Additionally, if you have the financial resources to fund your startup costs, the risk of starting the business would be minimal as your own financial resources are at stake and the full ownership of the business is under your control. When you utilize your own capital, you are in the position to make all the decisions and don't have to consult with others to make the decisions. If you have partners, and your partners contribute to the startup costs and expenses of the business, then the decisions of the business would have to be discussed and agreed upon amongst the business partners.

Venture capital firms are usually focused on creating an investment portfolio of businesses with high growth potential resulting in high rates of returns. Angel investors are wealthy individuals looking to put money in startup businesses. Depending on where you live, you can find local angel investors groups. Bank loans are a traditional form of securing startup capital for a business and the bank's criteria for qualifying for credit are clearly defined with the policies and loan provisions of a bank.

I was formerly a business banker with Citibank during my corporate world experience, and I recall that the ability to get businesses approved for loans wasn't an easy task. The process was identifying businesses that had a track record in business of at least three years, supported by tax returns from the business, as well as personal tax returns from the principal owners. The bank criteria were also contingent on the principal owners of the business having industry experience in the business in which they operated, in order to show the bank that the individuals running the business had experience, which would increase the probability of the business's success. Therefore, seeking startup capital at Citibank was difficult. Other banks don't have the same criteria; however, it's important to recognize that startup capital, regardless of the source, would come at an additional expense of interest to pay back the source of the capital. With Citibank, an established business that showed success for an extended period was more likely to get approved for a line of credit as opposed to a business seeking startup capital.

Seeking capital to start a business from family and friends is an option. With this option, it is important to understand that your relationship with your family members or friends can be at stake if the communication between all parties is not clearly defined, as well as if the provisions for paying back the money aren't in writing. In some cases, your family member may extend the startup capital without expecting you to pay it back. One thing you must be careful about in this instance is that gift taxes are applied to money exchanged between family members if it reaches a certain amount. In 2021, you can give up to $15,000 to someone in a year and generally not have to deal with the IRS about it. In 2022, this threshold is $16,000. If you give more than $15,000 in cash or assets in a year to any one person, you need to file a gift tax return.

To succeed as an entrepreneur, one must take risks. Therefore, if a family member or friend wants to assist you with your business venture, they must also be willing to take the risk of the business either succeeding or failing. When seeking assistance from family members or friends, if the money is not a gift, then it is recommended that a contract be written to specify the conditions of the financial resources, the return of capital provisions, and the length of time during which the repayment is expected. This will increase the success of the relationships between the entrepreneur and the family members and friends if the business isn't successful.

CHAPTER FOUR

TYPES OF BUSINESSES AND INDUSTRIES THAT CAN SUCCEED

"Don't let anyone convince you that your dream, your vision to be an entrepreneur, is something that you shouldn't do. What often happens is that people who are well-meaning, who really care for us, are afraid for us and talk us out of it".

— Cathy Hughes

After the thought of business startup and ownership enters one's mind, then the question comes as to what business model would be best or what industry would provide the best probability for success. As you recall from my earlier thinking, when an individual has experience in a particular industry and has mastered certain skills as a result of that experience, they can subsequently transition from an employee mindset to an entrepreneur mindset and potentially make more money for themselves, as opposed to working for someone else and fulfilling someone else's dreams. Thus, the business enterprise idea can begin to evolve.

There are a variety of business models that exist. Some examples are direct sales, retail sales, online sales, franchising, leasing, and affiliate marketing. Becoming a retailer is the most common business model around. Essentially, you have products—either your own or from manufacturers—and you sell them to consumers. This can be done in a physical store or as an e-commerce company. When determining which type of model to select, an individual must research the startup costs involved, the labor necessary to start the business, the factors necessary to run the business, and the hours of operation necessary to be successful in the business. A business model should answer important questions about your business and set out a strong vision for the business. The key components of a business model should include relating to your target customers, the market, the organization's strengths and challenges, the essential elements of the product, and how the product will be sold.

When I was let go from Merrill Lynch because of the global financial crisis in 2008, I decided to start a health and wellness business. I had previous sales and marketing experience for many years in the pharmaceutical industry; therefore, my understanding of the importance of maintaining and improving individuals' health gave me the idea that a health and wellness business was in alignment with my experience, knowledge base, and an industry I can succeed in. The ability to get the business started didn't require an enormous amount of capital, and the products to begin marketing the business were already established. The business model was a network marketing platform, which has its advantages and disadvantages, like most business models do. As my business generated income initially, because I was excited about assisting individuals with maintaining and improving their health, I saw an ability to transition from being an employee of a well-established company to becoming an entrepreneur in a direct sales environment. Having the confidence to sell any product or service is a result of my many years of professional sales experience in various industries spanning three decades. As I maintained the business, the profitability of the business increased gradually; however, it didn't provide enough income to meet all my monthly expenses after several months of marketing the health and wellness products through the direct sales model.

Ultimately, my passion for financial services and assisting individuals to secure their financial future through financial planning and wealth building strategies led me back into a role as a financial advisor and owner of my agency. However, it was a transitionary period during my return to financial services as I began to learn the Medicare business and became an employee at Healthfirst and UnitedHealthcare, marketing Medicare Advantage plans to seniors. These experiences were beneficial in that I learned a new skill and was able to leverage my existing Life and Health insurance license to work to meet my monthly expenses. The financial services industry was still experiencing major adjustments as a result of the global crisis; therefore, I was selective in which opportunity in the industry would be best suited for me to take advantage of. Overcoming adversity through experience and course-correcting during one's career requires an individual to take introspection and determine which path to take based on the circumstances presented to oneself.

Determining which industry to start your business enterprise in is a very important decision. As you ponder which industry is best, being passionate about what you'll be doing and having an enormous interest in what kind of product or service you'll be marketing is crucial to executing your business plan. In my opinion, some industries for aspiring individuals to consider starting a business in are the financial services, technology, healthcare, and sports and entertainment industries.

In a recent conversation with one of the top CEOs of a major consulting firm, Thomas Dortch, Jr., who also is the chairman of One Hundred Black Men of America, Inc., he shared with me some of the top industries in which he believes aspiring entrepreneurs can have a major impact post-pandemic. Mr. Dortch feels "the top industries are technology, cybersecurity, financial services, and home building for affordable housing." I'm happy that some of the industries Mr. Dortch feels are top industries are in alignment with the industries I believe aspiring entrepreneurs should consider.

You may ask why the financial services industry, especially knowing that the industry has its ups and downs and can be very risky at times. The financial services industry is a global industry that impacts the lives of many individuals. We live in a capitalistic society here in the U.S. and in most countries across the globe. With this being the case, capital and the movement of capital is an integral part of our daily lives; thus, we have decisions to make daily regarding capital. The industry continues to grow and expand; thus, when an individual pursues this industry to establish a career as either an employee of a major corporation or a business owner, they position themselves for a very lucrative career based on the opportunities that exist in the industry. Additionally, the industry is segmented in various disciplines, such as insurance, accountancy, corporate finance, investment banking, and financial planning. Having these various options to pursue specialization gives an individual an opportunity to select which discipline interests them the most, as well as which discipline can pay the most. We have an enormous wealth gap in our society; thus, individuals who can understand financial concepts, develop ways to grow their financial resources, and maximize wealth building strategies through the assistance of individuals who specialize in financial planning are able to lead rewarding lives. Those who are less fortunate to have the knowledge of financial concepts and assistance with building wealth are less fortunate, usually living paycheck to paycheck and remaining in the lower end of the wealth gap.

The financial services industry is worth $20.49 trillion worldwide. This was true as of 2020, and it was estimated that the industry would reach $22.52 trillion in value in 2021. The sector makes up approximately 20–25% of the global economy. The industry is expected to grow at a CAGR of 6% from 2020 to 2025, reaching $28.53 trillion in value at the end of that time period.

Source: U.S. Bureau of Labor Statistics Finance and Insurance NAICS

The U.S. financial services industry is worth about $4.85 trillion. This is the industry's revenue as of 2021, and it contributes $1.5 trillion to the U.S.'s total GDP, which ends up accounting for 7.4% of the total GDP. As far as the number of companies in the financial services industry is concerned, there are over 530,000 privates—and over 1,000 government—finance and insurance establishments that employ about 6.55 million people in the U.S. This is up from the 6.52 million people employed in 2021.

Source: SelectUSA Financial Services Spotlight: The Financial Services Industry in the United States

The technology industry presents a variety of opportunities and many distinct aspects of utilizing technology to establish major impacts within our society. As an individual thinks of developing a business focused on technology, one can choose from various segments of the industry. Some areas that come to mind regarding technological advances are Artificial Intelligence (AI), Machine Learning (ML), and Robotic Process Automation. Information technology is an area that covers cloud computing, mobile apps, big data analytics, automation, smart technology, and blockchain data. There are additional areas that will serve as emerging trends for years to come, and technological advances will continue to evolve. This presents an enormous number of options for aspiring entrepreneurs seeking entrepreneurial endeavors surrounding technology. Data's impact on technology is huge. Data allows organizations to determine the cause of problems more effectively. Additionally, data allows organizations to visualize relationships between what is happening in different locations, departments, and systems.

The technology industry is so broad and very lucrative; therefore, when considering focusing on solving problems, developing solutions, and increasing efficiency in our society, technological advancement is an important factor that will continue to create meaningful businesses within our society.

A leading consulting firm, Gartner, concludes that business priorities in the trends in 2023 will address certain areas. A recent observation from Gartner indicates. 2023 trends to impact enterprise strategies in the coming three years by enabling organizations to address four key priorities:

- Optimizing resilience, operation, or trust

- Scaling vertical solutions, product delivery or everywhere

- Pioneering customer engagement, accelerated responses, or opportunity ● Pursuing sustainable technology solutions

Source: Gartner – Insights/Information Technology, Article – October 2022

The technologies that are being maintained versus those that are driving the business are evident by their projected growth rates in 2023. There is sufficient spending within data center markets to maintain existing on-premises data centers, but new spending continues to shift to cloud options, as evidenced by the 11.3% projected growth for software spending in 2023 (see Table 1).

Table 1. Worldwide IT Spending Forecast (Millions of U.S. Dollars)

	2021 Spending	2021 Growth (%)	2022 Spending	2022 Growth (%)	2023 Spending	2023 Growth (%)
Data Center Systems	189,506	6.1	209,190	10.4	216,262	3.4
Software	732,030	14.8	790,385	8.0	879,625	11.3
Devices	807,580	15.8	739,982	-8.4	735,394	-0.6
IT Services	1,207,966	12.8	1,258,150	4.2	1,357,914	7.9
Communication Services	1,459,483	3.8	1,435,401	-1.7	1,469,220	2.4
Overall IT	4,396,565	10.2	4,433,108	0.8	4,658,416	5.1

Source: Gartner (October 2022)

The healthcare industry is a major part of our lives here in the U.S. and globally. Without good health and the maintenance of one's health, it's difficult to lead a basic, comfortable lifestyle. When an individual can establish good health and maximize their wealth, they can lead a gratifying lifestyle that enables them to travel, enjoy their family, and be productive in business and community service. Leading an active lifestyle additionally adds to one's longevity in life. The opportunities in the healthcare industry are vast and will continue to have a major impact on the lives of the masses. I've had an extensive career in the healthcare industry prior to transitioning to the financial services industry; therefore, I know the industry very well personally. As a result, I can attest to the industry's ability to represent a meaningful aspect of our daily lives. Additionally, I'm married to a healthcare administrator at a major hospital in the Bronx, New York.

Personally, I've become a health/wealth connection advocate, and thus, my ability to convey the importance of the health/wealth connection allows me to expand one of my ancillary businesses as a paid speaker. My public/keynote speaking business also gives me the ability to promote the books I've written, as individuals who have the privilege to become bestselling authors gain influence in industry and our respective communities. As I've been able to align my various skills to position myself as a thought leader in business, the financial services industry, and the healthcare industry, these experiences continue to provide me with opportunities to share my insights to the public, community-based organizations, churches, and professional organizations.

So, the takeaway message here is that when you gain experience in your specialized field and you're able to convey what you understand and provide your insights and opinions as to how you can make a difference or solve problems, your value as an individual increases. The more you're able to convey messages, thoughts, and solutions, you become someone the public looks to for guidance, and your perspective can assist them with problems they may be facing.

Key areas in healthcare that provide opportunities for aspiring entrepreneurs are limitless. As the aging population continues to increase, there will be an ever-evolving population of 65-plus-year-old individuals who will need care, services, and attention. The aging population coincides with the extensive trend of longevity in life. At the same time, as individuals age, the necessity for healthcare services will increase, as well.

Nationwide spending on health is projected to grow at an average rate of 5.5% annually through 2026. That's one percentage point faster than the national GDP is projected to grow during that same time. And by 2026, health care is projected to account for nearly 20% of the GDP.

A listing of potential health care business ideas to consider consists of:

1. Medical transcription services

2. Medical records management

3. Physical/occupational therapy center

4. Develop a health care app

5. Diabetic care center

6. Home health care service

7. Medical foot care

8. Drug treatment/rehabilitation center

Source: Nerwallet.com Article – Rieva Lesonsky – October 2022

This is just a partial listing of opportunities for aspiring entrepreneurs; therefore, you can imagine the continuous opportunities that exist in the healthcare industry. What's important to note is that these opportunities present lucrative income attainment probabilities, and some can be done by working remotely.

Another industry that is considered glamorous is the sports and entertainment industry. With the ever-evolving fan base for athletes and celebrities who make a living entertaining the public, there will continually be opportunities in this industry for aspiring entrepreneurs to develop business enterprises. As we watch sports and see entertainers perform, we are engaging in activities that bring us joy, pleasure, and atmospheres for socialization. When you think about the excitement of going to the stadium, ballpark, or concert venue, there is usually a feeling of anticipation, an expectation of a good time, and a feeling of relaxation because you'll be entertained.

Sports is a global business, and various sports leagues are finding ways to develop initiatives to expand their ability to grow their respective leagues and alliances. As sporting activities continue to expand, so do the businesses that support sporting events and contribute to the sporting venues. As entrepreneurs in this industry see the expansion, they can position themselves accordingly based on the opportunities available. Some areas of opportunity in the sports industry for entrepreneurs are medical treatment and rehabilitation, research and development, sports tourism, sales and trade of sports products, sports agents, construction of sporting venues, sales and marketing of sporting events, sports training, sports journalism, and franchise ownership.

With the recent passage of the new NIL law, which allows student athletes the ability to get compensated based on their name, image, and likeness, student athletes can now begin to pursue entrepreneurial endeavors before turning pro. As the landscape has changed in college sports as a result of this new law, enormous opportunities are now available for individuals who are able to develop themselves as a brand, create a business for themselves, and generate income to handle living expenses while still being students. For aspiring entrepreneurs who can guide these student athletes to navigate these newfound opportunities, lucrative income potential is available to them, as well.

When I think of the new opportunities for our young students, I'm reminded of my experience providing youth entrepreneurship training earlier in my career. I believe the earlier, the better to encourage and engage young people in the opportunities available to pursue entrepreneurial endeavors. When I also think of the competitive nature of athletes, I view them as perfect individuals to realize their full potential as entrepreneurs in addition to being superior athletes. The key takeaway message here is the importance of having a mindset of abundance, unlimited income potential, and a focus on building one's personal brand.

Sports have always been able to transcend "the game," serving to reflect on who we are as a society and offering a chance to see both our progress and our shortcomings. Sports organizations, teams, and players have embraced this role, and have influenced and improved their communities as a result. In 2022 and beyond, we will see the sports business continue to make progress, focusing more on the welfare of athletes, society, and the planet.

When establishing a business, raising capital, and securing startup costs is one of the greatest challenges entrepreneurs must contend with. With a variety of business models and platforms available to launch a business, if a business can open with low startup costs, an entrepreneur can then focus on executing the marketing and sales of the product or service. One model I would recommend individuals to consider is the direct sales business model. With this type of model, the entry point for beginning a business from a financial standpoint is manageable. At the same time, in many cases, the product or service is established, and a system is in place for the aspiring entrepreneur to duplicate. What is important to note in this scenario is that the aspiring entrepreneur must have excellent selling skills, people skills, consultative skills, leadership skills, and extreme listening skills. Effective listening is probably the most important skill an entrepreneur in the direct sales business should possess, as they would be charged with understanding the prospect's goals and objectives, dissatisfaction points, and needs assessment for the business's product or service.

Becky Launder, co-founder & CEO of Modern Direct Seller & Directflo and a thought leader in the direct sales industry, made a recent observation and stated, "While so many direct sellers are focused on the buzz around social selling, attraction marketing, and becoming the next influencer, it's a passive selling strategy and not actually getting results. For direct sellers to truly be successful in 2022, it is critical to focus on fine-tuning active selling strategies—by getting in front of new customers, building authentic relationships, having conversations, and actually selling. The post and pray method doesn't work. Building a direct sales business in 2022 takes work, and direct sellers need to develop the sales skills to be set up for success."

According to statistics from the Direct Selling Association, in 2021, there were 7.3 million direct sellers who built a business full time (30 or more hours per week) or part-time (fewer than 30 hours per week). These individuals sell products and services to consumers and may encourage others to become business partners with them to promote the products and services.

On the other end of the spectrum, if an aspiring entrepreneur chooses to start a business through a franchising opportunity, the cost of entry to this business model is hundreds of thousands of dollars in most instances. On the low end, a person may have to invest $20,000 to $30,000 for a franchising opportunity.

7 Mindsets To Successfully Transition From Employee To Entrepreneur

The Bureau of Labor Statistics reports that about 20% of independent businesses close after two years. In contrast, franchise consulting firm FranNet reports that 92% of franchisees were still going strong after two years. Therefore, one can conclude that franchising opportunities can be successful business ventures. At the same time, the capital investment to start can be expensive. The success rate of franchising ventures is due to the fact there is a proven system in place that is duplicated, and business owners have examples of previous franchise owners' practices, mistakes, and mentoring, which assists in their business development.

There is a necessity for careful thoughts and considerations for the aspiring entrepreneur as he or she imparts on starting a business venture. The ability to research an industry, determining what skills you are good at, and the growth trajectory of a potential product or service is key for you as a business owner. My experience as an entrepreneur has taught me that entrepreneurship is extremely rewarding, and at the same time, there are challenges that one must deal with to be successful. Once these challenges are handled, the rewards of being an entrepreneur are fulfilled. The ability to have a sustainable business is what God has envisioned most people to have. As you transition from an employee's mindset to an entrepreneur's mindset, your perspective will change as to the decisions you make and the commitment, you'll have for succeeding for you and your family. As you visualize, then realize that you are in business for yourself, you are now on the verge of building a legacy for yourself.

CHAPTER FIVE

DEVELOPING YOUR TEAM (MASTERMIND) OF ADVISORS

"*You are where you are today because you stand on somebody's shoulders. And wherever you are heading, you cannot get there by yourself. If you stand on the shoulders of others, you have a reciprocal responsibility to live your life so that others may stand on your shoulders. It's the quid pro quo of life. We exist temporarily through what we take, but we live forever through what we give*".

— Vernon Jordan

A s the saying goes, "Being in business for yourself, but not by yourself." This resonates so well with entrepreneurs and business owners. Regardless as to whether you're a sole-proprietor or president and CEO of your firm with employees and a management team, you'll need to assemble a team to surround yourself with to effectively manage and grow your business. Some members of your team will be internal, and others will be external members of your business whom you can seek advice from and collaborate with to enhance your business's success. Establishing a board of advisors of external thought leaders in business and industry can be very beneficial to you as you start and operate your business enterprise.

Members of your advisory board are there to provide guidance, offer recommendations, and be objective with you as you seek their advice to leverage their experience. It's important that you clearly define the mission of your organization, the goals you've established to grow your business, and the impact you wish to have on society. With this information, your advisory board can provide guidance in accordance with your vision. Your advisory board members can also assist you in determining whether your business objectives can be reached based on how your business is structured. These members can also be a source as collaborators in business, as they may provide products or services that your clients can utilize in conjunction with your product or service.

Seeking the advice of an attorney to establish your business and get you incorporated is a wise decision. Some entrepreneurs think of going into business, and they may want to save costs and incorporate their business on their own. Certainly, there are services available that you can utilize to incorporate your business, however, I recommend using an attorney to assist you, as the attorney can provide you with advice on the recommended structure to incorporate your business as. Different business structures have advantages and disadvantages when it comes to taxes. Additionally, if you develop a product and your invention requires a patent, then seeking out an intellectual property attorney is essential to protect the rights of your invention. Intellectual property must be protected accordingly. Lastly, as a business owner, you always want to have an attorney whom you can have access to for counsel, who is available to represent you and your business in case your business is faced with any legal issues.

Having an insurance broker available to provide insurance protection for your business is essential. Whether you have a brick-and-mortar location, or your business is online and accessible virtually, it's mandatory to have insurance protection for your business in case you are sued due to injury of clients at your business location. Disability insurance to protect you from loss of income due to injury is important, as well. Additionally, you must consider health benefits, as well as life insurance for you and your respective business partners if you are in partnership with other business owners. Establishing buy-sell agreements between you and your business partners to protect your business in case of the untimely death of you or one of your partners is an incredibly good practice.

Another key person to assemble as part of your team is a CPA or an accountant who is trained and has experience working with entrepreneurs and small business owners as they start their business. When a business owner has detailed books and can have excellent records of the business's revenue, expenses, profit and loss statements, taxes, and financial obligations internally and externally with the business, they are setting the business up for success. It is very critical to monitor the business growth and development and be able to understand the financials of the business from the start. This concise recordkeeping can make a difference with business reporting when it's time to pay taxes or secure credit in the future if the business owner would like to expand the business.

Another external partner is a licensed financial advisor who can provide you with wealth management strategies for you personally, as well as strategies for the business's assets. When business owners start out, they may not make a profit for the first few years. This is an area in which the business owner must manage the expectations of the time period it will take to become profitable. It's important, though, that retirement planning is a part of the goals for the business owner because many business owners are very focused on the profitability of the business, and they don't focus on the future and how putting money away or establishing investments for later in life is critical for securing one's financial future.

Creating an image for your business through public relations, marketing, and advertising provides your business the visibility to the public and prospective clients. As the role of a public relations professional is to establish and maintain a good public image and reputation of companies, it also helps to manage any negative publicity that companies may face. Therefore, public relations partners can build a company's reputation and reverse a company's bad reputation due to unforeseen circumstances. Public relations professionals work in tandem with marketing and advertising organizations. PR is intended to promote an organization, whereas marketing and advertising is focused on delivering the message of the brand, products, or services.

Today, social media has gained an enormous amount of importance with individuals, small business owners, and large corporations. Utilizing social media has become part of our daily lives. As a result, it's important to have a social media strategy in place as an aspiring entrepreneur. Establishing a social media presence and generating a huge following assists a business owner with brand awareness, brand image, and brand development. Having someone in your business manage social media strategies or hiring an external partner to handle these duties is something the business owner must decide on; however, it's important that a strategy is put in place to keep pace with your competitors.

An executive assistant is an internal role that is very important to the entrepreneur or business owner, as he or she is focused on running the business. There are some cases when an entrepreneur may have an external partner serve as an executive assistant with virtual responsibilities. Regardless as to whether the assistant works with the organization internally or externally, the role and responsibility of an executive assistant is vital to the success of the business owner. The duty of an executive assistant is to perform clerical and administrative tasks, including drafting letters, memos, invoices, reports, and other documents for the business. The assistant is also charged with making travel arrangements and accommodations when the owner may need to travel to meetings or conferences. Additionally, keeping an account of minutes from meetings and upcoming tasks the owner must fulfill is an assistant's responsibility.

As the business grows and expands, the business owner will seek to hire additional staff and begin to hire consistently to keep pace with the growth of the business. What's important to note is that as a business develops, the management of the staff needed to satisfy the demand for the products or services of the company is essential. If the demand for a company's products and services increases and the company isn't adequately equipped to meet the demand of the customer base, then that can create problems for the business. Having proper customer service for the clients is an ingredient for success in business. When there's a problem with customer service or supply of the product or service, then clients will seek products and services elsewhere—in most cases, from your competition. In order to maintain a competitive advantage, a business must be adequately supplied with inventory and properly staffed with individuals who deliver professional customer service. Therefore, management of the supply and demand is critical.

CHAPTER SIX

INTERVIEWS OF SUCCESSFUL ENTREPRENEURS

"Dedicate yourself to a core set of values. Without them, you will never be able to find personal fulfillment, and you will never be able to lead effectively".

— Kenneth Chenault

When thinking of the ability to launch a business and succeed through the various cycles of business formation, development, growth, and sustainability, it's important to gather an understanding from individuals who have done so. Therefore, I spent some time conversing with people who have experience as business owners after working in the corporate world and successfully making the transition to develop entrepreneurial endeavors. The experiences of these individuals can give you a clearer picture of the success, challenges, rewards, and what it takes to win in business. Some of these entrepreneurs still work in a corporation; however, they have a business enterprise, which gives them an additional stream of income to combine with their salary.

Alfred Edmond, Jr., SVP/Executive Editor-at-Large for *Black Enterprise*, is a professional with many years of experience in journalism, media, and publishing, serving as a public speaker and moderator for many events across the country. Additionally, Alfred is an author and radio show host, and provides coaching for aspiring entrepreneurs. While working with *Black Enterprise* many years ago, I had the privilege of working with Alfred as we developed and promoted Building Wealth conferences across the country to educate the community on wealth building strategies and financial literacy concepts. In conversations with Alfred, he shared insights with me that can give an aspiring entrepreneur a good understanding of the entrepreneurship process. Alfred was inspired to develop his entrepreneurial endeavors because he realized all industries have salary caps on individuals' earning potential. He concluded that to increase his earning potential, he would have to gain some time of his own to allow him to begin public speaking, developing podcasts, mentoring, and coaching clients.

Edmond advises aspiring entrepreneurs to know exactly what you want, and once you understand what you want, then you can get very good at the activities that bring you satisfaction and the life you want through your business endeavors. A challenge Alfred indicated he had to overcome as he began his entrepreneurial endeavors was understanding that as an employee, an individual has structure in place and a full-time assistant who provides operational support, along with administrative responsibilities and consistent pay through a salary. As an entrepreneur, he had to develop a system and handle various duties and responsibilities until he earned enough revenue or income to hire staff to assist with the aforementioned duties.

Alfred feels that to build a successful business, you, as a business owner, must build a system where you don't have to do everything yourself. By utilizing the collaborative efforts of others, with you serving as the conductor, a business enterprise can scale. "To reach the masses of people who can benefit from your product or services, entrepreneurs must incorporate technology, people, processes, and customer service in order to have a repeatable business model."

Brandi McAlister, Founder and CEO of Blessed by Brandi, Inc. and Pray the Impossible, is a dynamic entrepreneur, spiritual leader, and life coach who embodies success and an uplifting spirit. I've known Brandi for many years and have watched her develop into a leader in her community and an inspiration to her peers. In addition, Brandi is an author and reaches many individuals through the events she promotes, which enrich attendees' overall well-being, as well as their lives spiritually, mentally, physically, and financially. I've had the opportunity to partner with Brandi with a few events, and I can say that our collaborative efforts were phenomenally successful in providing our attendees with essential insights that they were able to implement to make improvements and changes in their lives. Brandi was inspired to venture into entrepreneurship while finishing her master's degree in Marketing Communications, and she authored a book, *Real Talk – 30 Day Devotional*. As Brandi was completing her book, she created a website to create a following for her book, and she needed a name for her site. She decided on Pray the Impossible, and thus, her non-profit organization was born as a result. Blessed By Brandi, Inc. soon followed as she wanted to share her message with the masses and give individuals the ability to grow personally and professionally by attending her events and enhancing their lives. Brandi transitioned to start her businesses after working in corporate America for many years, with her last position serving as a Project Manager. When COVID-19 hit our world, Brandi was laid off along with thousands of other people, this being the third time she was laid off from a position. With this last layoff, Brandi felt it was a signal from God that she takes the risk and venture into her entrepreneurial endeavor.

Ms. McAlister attributes her success as an entrepreneur to her ability to be authentic and relatable to many people, which gives people the feeling that she is genuine. Regarding challenges she has had to overcome to maintain her business, Brandi realized that with promoting events, it's a long sales cycle and, at times, attendees take their time with making commitments to attend events. This being the situation, her expectations were managed, especially when she promoted events that catered to the male population.

Brandi's advice for aspiring entrepreneurs is to maintain a level of consistency when operating a business and be patient with yourself through the process of developing your business. Additionally, she recommends surrounding yourself with other successful entrepreneurs to develop mastermind opportunities for the purpose of assisting in each other's growth. Certainly, focus on your self-care, as the rigors of entrepreneurship can be tough as times and individuals must prioritize their emotional, financial, and mental well-being. Lastly, focus on your process and don't give up.

Quentin Stephenson, President, and CEO of Senior Health Innovations, has a Medicare agency focused on assisting individuals with making sound decisions for their Medicare services. I've known Quentin for many years, as we spent time collaborating with one another as Quentin began learning the financial services business. During the time when Quentin sought advice and mentoring to better understand how to give adequate recommendations for his clients, he would ask my opinion on how I would make assessments for clients and their families. Through our collaborative business efforts, we would give seminars and educate prospective clients and members of the community about financial literacy concepts. Additionally, during some of our conversations, the topic of Medicare surfaced, and since I was Medicare certified, I was able to provide Quentin with guidance in that area. While starting his financial services business on a part-time basis, Quentin's full-time employment began to cause frustration for him because he felt trapped as a social services case worker. He went back to school for an advanced degree to get ahead in his profession; however, he wasn't making the progress in his career that he felt he deserved. The main area of frustration was the lack of freedom and flexibility of time because his case worker role required him to work extra hours, and when a client was faced with a crisis, Quentin had to ensure the situation was placed in control before he could leave work to tend to his familial obligations.

While learning the financial services business, Quentin's interest began to lean more towards the Medicare industry, and he developed a niche in the Medicare space; thus, the trajectory of his Medicare book of business began grow. Contracting with various carriers and diligently learning his craft in the Medicare space led Quentin to resign from his social services case worker position and dedicate his full time towards building a successful Medicare agency. While serving as a mentor to Quentin, I introduced him to one of my former colleagues in the Medicare industry, who subsequently began providing Quentin with additional guidance about the industry. Their collaborative efforts as business partners have led to immense success for them. Quentin shared the challenges he had to overcome to be successful as an agency owner, which were time management, building consistent income through following up on leads, and his ability to stay focused. He advises aspiring entrepreneurs to understand failure is a part of the process.

Additionally, an entrepreneur must learn everything about their business, pay their dues, and work from the bottom to eventually get to the top. Khalia Murray is currently a K-12 Implementation Specialist. She is a former teacher, and she is now also the Founder of Ms. Murray's Corner, an Atlanta-based tutoring company. Ms. Murray's Corner serves students in pre-kindergarten through second grade, focusing on literacy, math concepts, and reading comprehension. Khalia was inspired to pursue her entrepreneurial endeavor because of the pandemic. When the world was faced with the pandemic and teachers and students shifted to working virtually and receiving education from home, Ms. Murray decided to tap into her creative side to utilize technology and launch Ms. Murray's Corner. Initially, it started with her coaching and tutoring her nieces and nephews to assist her siblings as the world adjusted to the transition of working virtually. When her sister, T. Amiyra King, saw the work she was doing with her nieces and nephews, she recommended Khalia begin promoting her services beyond her family and friends because she felt the content was excellent and more students could benefit from her services.

Khalia attributes her success with her tutoring business to being able to work virtually to deliver her services and the benefit of having flexibility with her time, allowing her to serve students as she continues to maintain her career as a K-12 implementation specialist. The ability to leverage social media for promoting and marketing her services, as she was invited to be interviewed on podcasts, accelerated the growth of her business. With any business, there are certain challenges a business owner will face and must overcome. One of the challenges Khalia faced was when parents and students returned to work and school; she had to prioritize her time accordingly to be able to schedule delivering her tutoring services after her workday was over. Additionally, Khalia received feedback from a tutoring coach that the value of the services she was delivering was priced too low, and she was recommended to make an adjustment to price her services in line with the market value of the services.

Khalia advises aspiring entrepreneurs to have full confidence in yourself, be prepared to take the necessary risks to start your business and set goals for yourself to achieve revenue and profits for your business to succeed. She feels it's important to stay true to yourself and visualize your business growth being manifested expeditiously with support from your inner circle of advisors. The ability to make mistakes and learn from them will provide individuals with a foundation to build upon as the entrepreneurial endeavor is actualized.

Jasmine Barnett, CEO and Owner of Bloom & Groom Wellness Lounge, has been in business since 2015. Jasmine's business initially started as a mobile service, as she was still employed by Accenture in the Global Consulting division. While primarily servicing family and friends was the beginning of her enterprise, she had visions to expand her business and provide additional services to her client base. When her tenure at Accenture ended because of layoffs, Jasmine took a severance package and made the decision to put all her energy into her business; thus, she began providing services at a brick-and-mortar location in Bloomfield, New Jersey two years ago. Thus, her transition to entrepreneurship was gradual, which allowed

Jasmine to begin providing services, understand her market, and take her business to the next level by adding services based on the demand of her clients.

Initially, Bloom & Groom Wellness Lounge was servicing women; however, it was Jasmine's goal to provide services for men, as well. Therefore, she had to market to people simultaneously to ensure men knew they were welcomed, and the services provided were intended for them, too. I've had the opportunity to collaborate with Jasmine and Bloom & Groom Wellness Lounge by promoting events together in partnership with Blessed by Brandi, Inc., focused on mind, health, and wealth empowerment. I, being a health/wealth connection advocate focused on educating individuals and groups about the importance of health and wealth, saw that partnering with a likeminded professional like Jasmine was an excellent way to continue making an impact in the community by providing information to improve individuals' lives.

Jasmine attributes her success in business to being creative to cater to her clientele. Additionally, offering certain services has enabled her to continue the growth of her business, and partnering with other organizations has provided a tremendous boost to her business's bottom line. Promoting events in collaboration with Blessed by Brandi, Inc., nurses, and other wellness companies in the spa community has been a driving force to her success. Certainly, when the pandemic surfaced, it impacted her business. At the same time, Jasmine was able to overcome the challenges of the pandemic by educating people on setting boundaries when receiving services in person and ensuring social distancing was practiced diligently. The advice for aspiring entrepreneurs Jasmine would like to share is to invest in a business coach to assist with determining what's important to you as you develop your business and keep track of the progress of your business. Additionally, Jasmine feels it's important to establish an accountability partner and provide support for one another. Lastly, understand how to leverage business credit to grow and expand your business.

Imani J. Murray, President and CEO of FPL Unlimited, worked in the auto industry for many years and most recently served in an individual producing sales role at Audi, selling luxury cars to an affluent clientele. He was raised by an entrepreneur who continually encouraged and advocated the benefits of entrepreneurship as an option to build a successful career in business. As Murray excelled in his career in the auto industry, he developed superior sales skills and persuasive skills to reach top accolades within his tenure at Audi. When the pandemic surfaced here in this country and abroad, Imani was placed in a position which many others were faced with, and he subsequently had to transition and begin working for himself because his employer made the decision that his services at the dealership were no longer needed. Having to continue to raise his family, he sought out the ability to develop a business as a broker in the auto industry, and thus, his entrepreneurial venture was established.

Timing is everything, and in this case, the start of Mr. Murray's business as a broker was successful because the relationships already in place allowed him to leverage the relationships with individuals who he already serviced, who subsequently provided referrals to many individuals who were in the market for automobiles. The momentum of FPL Unlimited gave the business the necessary flow of business to increase the brand awareness of a new company who already positioned themselves as a customer service-oriented company. The overall salesmanship of Imani working in the industry led to his success in securing luxury vehicles to a market in demand.

As the pandemic forced supply chain issues for many industries, the auto industry was faced with the same challenges regarding supply of vehicles and parts to produce vehicles. This is one of the challenges FPL Unlimited had to overcome during the startup phase of the business. Additionally, Murray had to take control of other activities, such as operations, administrative duties, paying taxes, and acquiring vehicles to market to his customer base. Also, when inflation surfaced, which caused the price of vehicles to increase, Imani was forced to manage expectations of his customer base as he located the vehicles his clients were seeking. The insight Murray shared for aspiring entrepreneurs is the importance of having faith in yourself that you can go into business for yourself and be successful. A business owner must have adequate preparation for starting a business by developing a solid business plan and designing the plan accordingly to reach its targeted audience. Lastly, have the perseverance to weather the storms, peaks, and valleys of the journey of a successful entrepreneur.

Questions entrepreneurs should ask themselves when starting a business:

1. How long will it take for my business to reach profitability?

2. Who will I seek to serve as my board of advisors?

3. How will my business manage the challenges it will require to keep a sustainable business past five years?

4. What technology and support staff will be necessary for my business to operate through a systemic process?

5. Can my business outpace the competitors in the marketplace in the same industry, as well as compatible industries?

6. What type of budget is required for advertising and promotion to effectively market my business's products or services?

7. Which organizations can I seek to leverage for information, resources, and guidance to monitor my business's progress and develop growth strategies?

ENTREPRENEUR'S SPOTLIGHT

As you've heard from some outstanding entrepreneurs—a few who have fully transitioned to become entrepreneurs and lead successful businesses, and others who have maintained their roles in their respective companies while also having business enterprises—supporting businesses is essential for a business to grow and have sustainable business activity. I wanted to provide you with how you can contact these amazing entrepreneurs and learn more about the businesses they operate.

Photo Credit: Mary Brown/Mary Brown Photography & Design

Alfred Edmond, Jr., SVP/Executive Editor-at-Large, Black Enterprise www.blackenterprise.com/beyondthehype

www.blifteduparadio.com

IG: @alfrededmondjr

@BLiftedUpRadio

Jason S. Murray

Photo Credit: Brian Johnson/Mr. Brian Johnson Photography

Brandi McAlister, Founder

Pray the Impossible

www.praytheimpossible.com

IG: @praytheimpossible FB: Pray the Impossible

Blessed by Brandi, Inc. www.blessedbybrandi.org
info@blessedbybrandi.org

IG: @blessedbybrandi_inc

Quentin Stephenson, President & CEO, Senior Health Innovations, Inc. www.seniorhealthinnovations.com

quentinrstephenson@seniorhealthinnovations.com

Photo Credit: Jade Bynum /@MomentsWithJade

Jason S. Murray

Khalia Murray, Implementation Specialist, Everfi

www.everfi.com

Founder, Ms. Murray's Corner

www.msmurrayscorner.com

msmurrayscorner@gmail.com

IG: @msmurrayscorner

Photo Credit: Brian Johnson/Brian Johnson Studio

Jasmine Barnett, CEO & Owner, Bloom & Groom Wellness Lounge

www.bloomandgroomwellness.com

bloomandgroomwellness@gmail.com

IG: @bloomandgroomwellness

FB: Bloomandgroomwellness

Photo Credit: Brian Johnson/Brian Johnson Studio

Imani J. Murray, President & CEO, FPL Unlimited Auto

www.fplunlimitedauto.com

info@fplunlimitedauto.com

IG: @fplunlimited

CHAPTER SEVEN

DESCRIPTIONS AND HOW TO CREATE BUDGETS/MARKETING/PROFIT FORECASTING/BUSINESS PLAN/COMPETITIVE ANALYSIS

"I'm hungry for knowledge. The whole thing is to learn every day, to get brighter and brighter. That's what this world is about. You look at someone like Gandhi, and he glowed. Martin Luther King glowed. Muhammad Ali glows. I think that's from being bright all the time. Be brighter".

— Jay Z

As we have heard from successful entrepreneurs, leaders, and business coaches, developing a sustainable business requires vision, strategic planning, forecasting, market research, competitive analysis, financial resources, and a comprehensive business plan. Regardless of the best constructed plans and strategies put in place, an entrepreneur must understand the fact that your strategies may have to be adjusted or modified as the business evolves over a time period.

What is the vision of your business? Developing a vision for your business assists an entrepreneur with understanding the direction of your enterprise, enabling you to focus in on who you want to provide products or services for and who can benefit from your products or services. Therefore, identification of your target market is an essential step in business formation.

Opening a business requires financial resources, and to operate a business effectively, it will require ongoing financial resources to properly keep the operation of the business flowing. Establishing a budget for the necessary startup costs are a very critical element in the creation of a business. A budget for a business consists of several items. Factors within a budget for a business include fixed expenses, variable expenses, sources of capital, break-even point, and revenue projections. Some examples of fixed costs would be rent or lease payments, costs to produce a product or deliver a service on a monthly basis, business insurance expenses, utilities, and salaries if staff is hired to run the business. Some examples of variable expenses are advertising and promotion, distribution costs, bookkeeping, and accounting expenses, as well as telecommunication expenses. The initial startup costs can come from one or more sources. Many entrepreneurs must use their own source of savings to capitalize their initial business formation. At times, individuals will utilize their retirement account savings as a source for the startup costs for their business. This isn't the most economical way of starting a business, especially if the individual is under 59 ½ and is subjected to paying taxes and penalties on the early distribution of retirement account resources. If an individual is fortunate to get a loan for the startup costs, a factor which must be taken into consideration is that the money must be paid back with interest. The SBA is a great resource and provides many guides and templates to calculate startup costs for a business. The following link is a source for calculating startup costs:

https://www.sba.gov/business-guide/plan-your-business/calculate-your-startup costs

It's one thing to start a business. The area which many entrepreneurs don't put enough emphasis on is marketing your business to the public. If your potential customers aren't aware, you are in business or don't know where to find you for your business's products or services, then you will be left with a lot of inventory at the end of the month. Therefore, developing an effective marketing plan is crucial for the success of your business enterprise. A marketing campaign can be implemented using various mediums to get your message out and begin building brand awareness. Marketing is the effective way of sharing who you are, what your business offers, how you can serve your client base with the products or services you offer, and why individuals would want to do business with you.

Various available vehicles can be utilized to get your message to your target market audience. Some examples are direct mail, email marketing, magazines, networking, newspaper, promotional materials, public relations, radio, telemarketing, and online marketing. Direct sales are a method of marketing which provides a business with the most control over the outcome when marketing a product or service because you have direct contact with the clients, and they will either purchase your product or service or decline based on the effectiveness of the approach used to convey the features and benefits. With utilizing these various mediums and vehicles for marketing, there will be advantages and disadvantages with each; therefore, a business owner must determine which medium is most effective based on the response rate, the success rate, and the costs associated with utilizing each medium.

To establish an effective marketing strategy through an effective plan of action, it's important to thoroughly determine your messaging, goals, outcomes, reach, and coverage points. There are several resources available to assist a business owner with developing a marketing plan. Below is a link for a template which can be utilized:

https://blog.hubspot.com/marketing/marketing-plan-template-generator

Individuals go into business for different reasons. One reason is constant with most business owners: The entrepreneur wants to establish a business that will eventually be profitable. Profitable business establishment requires hard work, strategic planning, and the ability to execute your business objectives consistently. The equation for a profit in business is very simple:

Revenue – (Fixed Costs + Variable Costs) = Profit

The goal for businesses is to reach a level of profitability as quickly as possible, enabling the business to reinvest the profits and continue producing the products or services the business offers to its client base, while continuing to expand the business's client base. The profit/loss statement gives the business a clear understanding of the direction of the business and allows the ownership of the business to see if the business objectives are being achieved. Earlier in this book, we discussed that it could take years for businesses to reach a level of profitability, and in some cases, some businesses never make a profit. As the business goals are driving forces to keep the leadership of the company focused, at times, unforeseen circumstances occur, and the ownership must further assess the direction of the company or adjust in marketing, promotion, and public relations to give the business the best opportunities to succeed. Therefore, it is particularly important to properly forecast when the company should be able to make a profit based on market research, supply and demand analysis, and a clear understanding of the competitive analysis from the company's competition.

In addition to a profit/loss statement, there are other statements and reports that can be organized and established for the ownership of a company to prepare to give an analysis of the business. The link below provides various templates for business use:

https://www.jotform.com/pdf-templates/business

A company's business plan is the blueprint for the execution of the company's goals and objectives. When creating a business plan, various factors are taken into consideration for the organization of the plan, the scope of the plan, and the outcome of the plan. A company can choose to develop a simple business plan or a very comprehensive plan to meet the company's objectives. Regardless of how detailed the plan is, it's important that the plan is structured for success and the ability to adjust if necessary is available. This gives the leadership of a company the flexibility to make changes and adjust accordingly if course correction will increase the probability of successful outcomes.

An executive summary of a business plan highlights some brief areas of the plan, which may include your mission and vision statements, in addition to an outline of your strategy, financial information, and projections. Components of the business plan may include company description, management and personnel of the company, market analysis, products and services, marketing plan, operations plan, and financial plan. As the business generates revenue, the execution of the business plan is intended to increase the revenue of the company.

A company's goal is to gain as much market share as possible. When creating a business plan for a company, the competitive analysis is a crucial part of the plan. Competitors in a marketplace focus their energy on understanding the competition, determining how their company can compete with their competitors and what is your company's unique value proposition. Competition is particularly good for business, as it assists in the expansion of a market. Market share at stake in a competitive environment drives the leaders of a company to develop certain features and benefits, which prospective clients will see as valuable. Therefore, the competitive analysis process will determine how a company will create the marketing and promotion of their respective products or services, keeping in mind that the acquisition of market share drives business revenue.

Jason S. Murray

The decision to go into business requires tremendous planning, and the rewards of a successful business enterprise provides an entrepreneur with a feeling of accomplishment. As I have transitioned from employee to entrepreneur, I can attest to the feeling of accomplishment, as I've led a successful business enterprise for many years. During the process, I've learned from others who have paved the way for me to be successful. I've also seen what it takes to persevere throughout the process because entrepreneurship is a journey of peaks and valleys, then additional peaks and valleys. To be successful with any entrepreneurial endeavor, it's important to maintain a level of strength, have an ability to adapt to various conditions, and have unwavering persistence throughout the journey. My corporate world work experience and volunteer service experience as a leader in professional non-profit organizations certainly prepared me for my life as an entrepreneur. I encourage individuals who are interested in pursuing entrepreneurial endeavors to think it through before venturing into the business formation process, as the ability to succeed isn't easy, yet the outcome of a sustainable business enterprise will create a phenomenal feeling of accomplishment.

CHAPTER EIGHT

CONCLUSION

When thinking of writing this book, I reflected on the feedback received from individuals who read my first publication, *Faith+Purpose=Legacy*. Readers wanted more, and they expressed that my shared insights were very welcomed. At the same time, they wanted to know more about how to start a business and what it would take to bring a business idea to fruition. Therefore, this book is intended to provide individuals with a blueprint to assess their preparation to transition from an employee mindset to an entrepreneurial mindset and successfully start, own, and operate a profitable business. Since I came from an extensive background in sales and marketing, with business opportunities throughout my career while working in a corporate environment, it allowed me to convey insights in this book through personal experiences and from successful entrepreneurs who made the transition themselves.

Today, we are experiencing tremendous change in our society—shifts in how we work and how we receive services. Products and services aren't only provided through retail stores and at brick-and-mortar locations. They are provided online, and business is done virtually today at a greater rate based on the recent pandemic, which has changed our lives dramatically. With all the changes occurring with how we live, work, receive services, and deliver services, it's important that individuals pursuing entrepreneurial endeavors understand and adequately prepare for doing business differently and in accordance with how the changes have affected how we lead our lives. As a business owner, if you aren't adaptable to change, but your competition is adaptable to change, you are in jeopardy of losing business as a result.

While pursuing becoming an entrepreneur, I believe the best option is to gather information based on the idea you have for starting a business, build upon the idea through due diligence, determine what you are good at, complete a comprehensive business plan, gather the financial resources to begin the business, and then transition to working the business while still employed. As you implement your business plan, begin obtaining revenue from your business, and replace your income from the salary you receive from your job, following these steps will provide you with a ramp-up period to allow you to transition successfully to your entrepreneurial endeavor.

There are various options for business ideas and various platforms to pursue to become an entrepreneur; therefore, there shouldn't be limitations for individuals who have a goal to go into business. When faced with the option to stay in a work environment you are unhappy with versus taking the risk to pursue entrepreneurial endeavors, making the decision to seek a more satisfying environment is certainly a good choice. Today, so many people decide to stay in unhappy situations just to make ends meet, as opposed to having faith in themselves that they can succeed by venturing into business for themselves. The goal of this book is to provide individuals with the confidence necessary to see themselves in business, living the lives they want to lead and having the ability to build legacies for themselves and their families.

I can attest that entrepreneurship isn't easy, and when faced with the decision to give up or stick with it, some people will give up and return to working at a job again, while others will find a way to make the business work, despite the challenges they may be faced with. When it's time for mental toughness to keep an individual going, an individual is certainly happy that they stick with the process and endure whatever adversity they may be faced with. Having a support system, a board of advisors, and mentors along the way assists entrepreneurs with staying in business and providing solutions to keep the business operating. For those who may decide to return to being an employee, that's okay, as well. If the decision to return to working as an employee is in the best interests of you and your family, you shouldn't feel as though you've failed. You should be proud that you fulfilled your mission of becoming an entrepreneur; you reached a goal and accomplished something many people haven't achieved. Some individuals will maintain a job with a consistent salary and have a business as another source of income, thus having multiple streams of income. The takeaway message here is that individuals must do what is in their best interests and not feel as though one way is better than the other. The best way of working and earning a living is whatever scenario fits your goals, dreams, and objectives.

I certainly believe in multiple streams of income. When having an income or revenue stream through a business, it will fluctuate based on the activities and sales of the products or services of the business. With a fluctuating income stream, it's important to put money aside or develop a reserve account to enable your business to have a cushion in case there is a slowdown in your business during a certain part of the business cycle. Business expansion will occur when a business owner is capable of reinvesting in the business and providing opportunities for growth by adding product lines or services, which increases the revenue of the company. Adding an ancillary business to an existing business will provide the business owner with another source of income while continuing to build the primary business. It's important to focus on adding a business that is synergistic with your existing business to prevent the business owner's focus being centered in opposing directions.

I've been successful in developing an income stream from my primary business in the financial services industry while simultaneously becoming a bestselling author, which provides me with additional opportunities for sales and marketing consulting services. Together with my synergistic activities, I'm able to build upon one business after the other and continue to focus on my priorities as a financial services entrepreneur.

The ability to build my ever-evolving legacy is being fulfilled, and I'm grateful for the opportunities that have been paved for me through the mentors, board of advisors, and thought leaders in business I've been associated with throughout my career. My children have followed me to become entrepreneurs, homeowners, and leaders in their respective communities; thus, they've watched, learned, and implemented wealth-building strategies for themselves to properly take care of their families.

This book is published by my daughter's publishing company, Journal Joy Publishing, which is a true testament of an example of legacy. My mother, Elizabeth Murray, was a co-author of a book before I became an author. Subsequently, after I published my first book, my daughter, T. Amiyra King, began publishing books for my grandchildren, Aspen King, and Chandler King, who are authors. Thus, our family serves as an example that we understand generational wealth and passing down our talents and attributes to the next generation.

I sincerely thank you for your support in reading this publication. My goal is that the content of this book gives you the courage to take the leap of faith and fulfill your entrepreneurial aspirations.

I'm available to speak at events, conduct workshops, and provide insights at companies, community-based organizations, schools, and churches. My experience as a leader in training sales teams based on my corporate experience and as an entrepreneur in the financial services industry is well-documented.

Contact Jason Murray at the below website.

www.jasonsmurray.com

AUTHOR BIO

Jason Murray, is a father, grandfather, entrepreneur, community servant, organizational leader and author. Raised in the Bronx, NY by a single parent, Murray achieved scholastic success in school and developed business skills, marketing acumen and consultative aptitude in the corporate world which spanned three decades, working in the consumer goods, publishing, pharmaceutical, healthcare and financial services industries. The corporate world gave Jason the ability to foster and develop numerous relationships nationally and instilled in him the importance of business expansion and economic development through challenging experiences and consistent career advancement. Now, currently a serial entrepreneur, consultant and thought leader, Murray is charged with providing a blueprint for success by strengthening communities and narrowing the wealth gap through entrepreneurship education, leadership skills development and spiritual growth. Murray is a graduate of Marist College, with a B.S in Business Administration and a Concentration in Marketing. He additionally holds the Series 7, Series 66 and Life & Health

Insurance licenses. Jason became a widower at an early age, thus was a single parent himself for 3 years. He currently resides in Teaneck, NJ with his wife, Tanya. He raised six children through a blended family and has eleven grandchildren, which gives him a clear understanding of his ever- evolving legacy!

Contact Jason Murray at the below website.

www.jasonsmurray.com

RESOURCES

As I think of opportunities to share about organizations and individuals who represent excellence, leadership, and community service, I would like to acknowledge National Sales Network and Melanie Cook.

National Sales Network prepares individuals focused on sales and marketing as a career, to assist them with advancing in their career.

Melanie Cook is a well-sought-after CEO, leader and community servant who is a very accomplished conference speaker.

NSN 30TH ANNIVERSARY!!!

National Sales Network (NSN) Founded 1992, in Newark, NJ, is a not-for-profit membership organization whose objective is to meet the professional and developmental needs of sales professionals. NSN has also conducted an annual conference & career fair since 1996. The conference is attended by 2,000 + people from all major metro areas nationwide.

www.SalesNetwork.org

CPSIA information can be obtained
at www.ICGtesting.com
Printed in the USA
BVHW052102210423
662798BV00011BA/541